FOR YOUR HOME

LIVE-IN KITCHENS

FOR YOUR HOME

LIVE-IN KITCHENS

ELLEN M. PLANTE

FRIEDMAN/FAIRFAX
PUBLISHERS

Acknowledgments

With very special thanks to my editor, Reka Simonsen, of Michael Friedman Publishing Group, Inc.

A FRIEDMAN/FAIRFAX BOOK

Library of Congress Cataloging-in-Publication Data

Plante, Ellen M.
    Live-In Kitchens / by Ellen M. Plante.
        p.   cm.   — (For your home)
    Includes bibliographical references and index.
    ISBN 1-56799-719-8 (pbk.)
    1. Kitchens. 2. Interior decoration.   I.Title. II. Series
NK2117.K5P63 1999
643'.3—dc21   99-18452
                                                    CIP

Editors: Reka Simonsen and Hallie Einhorn
Art Director: Jeff Batzli
Designer: Jennifer S. Markson
Photography Editors: Wendy Missan and Amy Talluto
Production Manager: Richela Fabian

Color separations by Fine Arts Repro House Co., Ltd.
Printed in Hong Kong by Midas Printing Limited

1 3 5 7 9 10 8 6 4 2

For bulk purchases and special sales, please contact:
Friedman/Fairfax Publishers
Attention: Sales Department
15 West 26th Street
New York, New York 10010
212/685-6610 FAX 212/685-1307

Visit our website:
www.metrobooks.com

Page 2: Reminiscent of the colonial-era hall, this live-in kitchen is undoubtedly the heart of the home. A wood-beamed ceiling and a terra-cotta tile floor imbue the space with a rustic feeling. Architectural styling that resembles a fireplace mantel suggests that the stove area is the modern-day equivalent of a grand hearth.

CONTENTS

INTRODUCTION

Any kitchen, by virtue of its nature, is a designated work space. A live-in kitchen, whether of the "great room" variety or in the form of a spacious kitchen/dining area, combines the practical work of meal preparation with an opportunity to entertain, visit with the children, or simply enjoy the quiet company of others.

It's interesting to note that the live-in kitchen is by no means a modern concept; it is a design that's centuries old, a testament to the fact that a good idea never goes out of style. Our forebears enjoyed the warmth of the hearth in an all-purpose "hall" that served as both a kitchen and living area. Foods were prepared, clothes were mended, family prayers were said, and meals were shared in a single living space. While it has a romantic ring to it, this "hall" was actually necessary for survival. In the pre-petroleum age, life revolved around—and was dependent upon—the burning embers and warmth of the hearth. Homes were small and sufficient for the occupants' basic needs.

As homes grew larger, rooms became activity-specific, and from the late eighteenth century through the nineteenth century, the kitchen was considered a workroom. During this period, the parlor was the hub of family life, and domestic servants occupied the kitchen in many upper- and middle-class homes. By the early 1900s, the introduction of electric appliances and modern gadgetry transformed the kitchen into a domestic laboratory of sorts. Women, who by this point did most of their own housework, were still isolated from the rest of the family since the kitchen was usually located at the rear of the house, well removed from the social spaces in the home. This trend continued, but architectural designs of the 1920s and 1930s often included a "breakfast nook" adjacent to the kitchen that housed an enamel-top table and matching chairs for casual family meals. Several factors combined during the 1960s and 1970s to place greater emphasis on kitchen design and on the kitchen itself as a true living space—what we've come to call the heart of the home.

Opposite: THIS COMBINATION KITCHEN/DINING SPACE NOT ONLY ACCOMMODATES MORE THAN ONE COOK, BUT ALSO PROVIDES A SPOT WHERE GUESTS CAN RELAX AND CHILDREN CAN WORK ON SCHOOL PROJECTS. A VAULTED CEILING ADDS DRAMA, HEIGHTENING THE SPACIOUS FEELING OF THE ROOM, WHILE TWO SETS OF FRENCH DOORS SEEM TO EXTEND THE KITCHEN'S BOUNDARIES OUTDOORS. THE LINK TO THE OUTSIDE IS FURTHER ENHANCED BY TWO WICKER CHAIRS POSITIONED AT EITHER END OF THE TABLE.

Over the past three decades, the kitchen has come full circle, thanks to open-living floor plans and the renovation of commercial buildings for private use. In addition, the emergence of country-style interiors during the 1970s looked to the past to fashion inviting spaces for simplified living. The centuries-old "hall" inspired the combination kitchen/living areas that we've come to call great rooms.

The live-in kitchen, a multifunctional space that has become the cornerstone of so many homes, is first and foremost a work center and as such requires careful planning for maximum efficiency and ease. Traffic flow, adequate storage space, and comfortable workstations are important considerations for making any kitchen a success, but perhaps more so when designing a live-in kitchen, where everything is on view and people gather together. A convenient floor plan or design that routes traffic around or away from kitchen work areas will mean that no one is underfoot when the cook is preparing a meal.

When it comes to storage, you can never have too many kitchen cabinets. Abundant cupboard space in the live-in kitchen will tame clutter and give your work area a crisp, organized appearance. Regardless of whether you select stock cabinetry, custom-crafted cabinets, or free-standing cupboards or armoires that offer a "furnished" rather than "equipped" look, it pays to give considerable thought to storage needs beforehand. And think beyond your typical cabinetry—today there are numerous options, including swing-out pantry cupboards, appliance cupboards with electrical outlets, and large islands with extra storage space.

There are several work-area designs to select from when planning the layout for a live-in kitchen. Each takes into consideration the placement of the stove, refrigerator, and sink, which should be a comfortable distance from one another. One of the most practical choices is a U-shaped

Left: HERE'S A PERFECT EXAMPLE OF ALL THE BEAUTY, SPACE, AND COMFORT THAT A LIVE-IN KITCHEN AFFORDS. A CENTER ISLAND NOT ONLY DIVIDES THE OPEN SPACE BUT INCLUDES A GENEROUS TILED OVERHANG AND BAR CHAIRS, WHERE GUESTS CAN PERCH WHILE VISITING WITH THE COOK OR CHILDREN CAN ENJOY SNACKS.

kitchen that opens onto a family room or dining area but prevents congestion in the cook's territory. An island can be incorporated to create extra work space and to encourage guests to stay on the other side of the cooking zone, perhaps seated on stools at the island. A U-shape is also ideal for a large kitchen because it makes for shorter distances between appliances—especially if the range top or sink is located in the island.

An L-shaped kitchen, with the stove and sink placed along one wall and the refrigerator on the other, is a convenient layout in a spacious live-in kitchen that has a bank of windows or French doors. With plenty of room for dining or for a family area, an L-shaped kitchen keeps the cook at the center of all activity. In contrast, galleys (or single-wall plans) and corridor kitchens are typically used in smaller spaces, but even these work plans can incorporate a cozy dining space or comfortable sitting area. No matter what size your live-in kitchen, the key is to plan for optimum efficiency, convenience, and the needs of your particular lifestyle.

Above: THE GALLEYLIKE WORK AREA IN THIS MODERN KITCHEN WAS DESIGNED FOR EFFICIENCY—NOT AS A RESULT OF A LACK OF SPACE. THE REFRIGERATOR AND SINK ARE POSITIONED AGAINST THE FAR WALL, WHILE THE RANGE IS LOCATED IN THE ISLAND. RECESSED SHELVES FOR STORAGE AND AN OPEN FLOOR PLAN THAT ROUTES TRAFFIC AWAY FROM THE WORK AREA ENHANCE THE SENSE OF SPACE. WHIMSICAL LIGHTING FIXTURES ABOVE THE BREAKFAST BAR ADD DISTINCT PERSONALITY.

OPEN KITCHEN DESIGNS

While an open kitchen is generally a combined kitchen/dining area or a great room—an open-living floor plan that includes kitchen, dining, and living areas all in one—there are other interpretations of a live-in kitchen worth considering. Depending upon your lifestyle and the elements required to meet your family's needs, the live-in kitchen may also function as a home office, an entertainment center, or a sunroom; it may even include a greenhouse.

When it comes to planning an open kitchen design, there are several things to consider. Are you adding on to your home or remodeling an existing space for better efficiency? Will you have to tear down walls to increase the kitchen's size? And what about the family budget for such a project? An architect or contractor can help with this initial planning phase and guide you through the maze of load-bearing walls, plumbing, and electrical needs. A professional can also steer you in the right direction when architectural integrity is a concern.

In smaller homes without a formal dining room, a combination kitchen/dining area or a kitchen with an adjoining breakfast room can easily become the heart of the home with careful planning and attention to detail. This particular type of live-in kitchen benefits from French doors leading to a backyard patio or a generous bank of windows that floods the room with natural light, making it appear more open and spacious. An island, ideal in almost any kitchen, is a practical and decorative addition to a combination kitchen/dining area, since it not only routes traffic but creates a boundary between the two separate areas. Islands can also do double duty as breakfast bars for meals on the run, and they can provide storage space for everything from cookbooks and wine bottles to small appliances and kitchen linens.

While the majority of kitchen/dining areas are furnished with a handsome table and chairs, there are alternatives that can make the live-in kitchen more inviting and comfortable. For example, a window seat not only can be

Opposite: Casual meals are a snap when served at this handsome, custom-crafted island, which shows that beauty does not have to be sacrificed for convenience. While this kitchen was designed for a family on the go, close attention was paid to decorative details. The cabinetry incorporates furniturelike appointments, a grand arched window offers architectural drama, and warm wood flooring evokes the spirit of days gone by.

used for seating at the table but can be relished as a favorite spot to curl up with a cup of coffee and a good book as well. Or what about incorporating an L-shaped banquette that keeps the table closer to the wall and increases available floor space?

Above: A SMALL SPACE CAN STILL BE BIG ON STYLE. THIS COZY NICHE PROVES IDEAL FOR A WINDOW SEAT WITH A FIRST-RATE VIEW. COLORFUL THROW PILLOWS ADD COMFORT AND HELP TURN THE NOOK INTO THE PERFECT SPOT TO PERUSE THE MORNING PAPER.

The great room is ideal for those who enjoy an open-living floor plan. Three separate areas with different functions are open to one another, which makes this type of live-in kitchen perfect for families with small children or homeowners who enjoy a fair amount of entertaining. It is also ideal for vacation homes. A great room isn't necessarily lacking when it comes to architectural interest—far from it. Soaring cathedral ceilings, fireplaces, large decorative windows, and French doors all contribute notable style and architectural embellishment. Weight-bearing or purely decorative columns, rustic wooden trusses, and ceiling arches can also be incorporated to help define the different sections.

In addition to offering abundant kitchen, dining, and living space, the great room affords the opportunity to include task-specific sites suited to individual needs and interests. One popular option is a home office, incorporated into the designated kitchen area by adding a desk, an extra counter, or a computer cupboard that matches the kitchen cabinetry. In the "living" portion of the great room, a sizable entertainment center can help tame clutter by providing a single location for home electronics, videos, and compact discs.

Other live-in kitchens might be planned to take full advantage of a sunny location or the beauty of the great outdoors. One fashionable design combines a kitchen with an adjoining sunroom that serves as a cozy sitting area. With a lovely bank of windows or French doors, the kitchen/sitting room becomes a cheery, light-filled area with a view of the garden, backyard, or cityscape. Once again, an island—or perhaps an L-shaped extension of the counter—can designate space for meals, and a sunroom sofa can coax family or friends to relax while visiting with the cook. Definitely smaller than a great room but equally inviting, a live-in kitchen remodeled or designed with a sunroom can be the perfect means for achieving a family-friendly space.

For the avid gardener, a live-in kitchen that incorporates a greenhouse room brings the outdoors inside and puts a truly personal stamp on the home. French doors are an attractive option in a greenhouse room, and they can be closed and curtained during cooler weather to conserve heat. In warmer climates or during spring, summer, and early autumn, these doors can be left open, thereby extending the kitchen and family living space. Greenhouse rooms can be used as dining or sitting areas where family and friends are surrounded by lush plants and flowers. Even the tools of the gardener's trade—a workbench, clay pots, a watering can—become decorative elements that enhance a nature-inspired theme.

No matter which kind of live-in kitchen you prefer, combining a kitchen work area with space for other household activities will not only increase the value of your home but make it a more comfortable family haven—a concept that's increasingly important in today's fast-paced world.

Above: THIS BRIGHT AND SUNNY KITCHEN HAS BEEN DESIGNED TO TAKE FULL ADVANTAGE OF THE GREAT OUTDOORS. A GREENHOUSELIKE BANK OF WINDOWS PROVIDES PLENTY OF LIGHT FOR THIS GENEROUS SPACE, WHICH FEATURES GLASS-FRONT CABINETS, A SLEEK COUNTER FOR CASUAL MEALS, AND A RUSTIC DINING TABLE.

Above: THIS SPACIOUS GREAT ROOM SERVES A MULTITUDE OF PURPOSES. FAMILY MEMBERS OR GUESTS CAN SIT ON STOOLS PLACED AROUND THE COUNTER WHILE A MEAL IS PREPARED, THEN MOVE TO THE DINING TABLE FOR AN ELEGANT FEAST. A SIZABLE WINDOW SEAT NOT ONLY OFFERS THE PERFECT SPOT TO WIND DOWN AND ENJOY THE SUNNY VIEW, BUT ALSO INCORPORATES HANDY DRAWERS FOR KEEPING TABLE LINENS WITHIN EASY REACH.

Above: CLASSIC ARCHITECTURAL DETAILS BRING TIMELESS BEAUTY TO THIS LIVE-IN KITCHEN. HANDSOME COLUMNS AND A RAISED HARDWOOD FLOOR SEPARATE THE KITCHEN FROM THE FAMILY ROOM AREA WITHOUT DETRACTING FROM THE SPACIOUSNESS OF THE OPEN DESIGN. WHITE CABINETRY COMPLETE WITH DECORATIVE CROWN MOLDINGS REINFORCES THE TRADITIONAL DECORATING SCHEME.

Opposite: THIS LIVE-IN KITCHEN ACCOMMODATES BOTH FORMAL AND CASUAL DINING WITH EASE. A FREESTANDING, CUSTOM-CRAFTED CUPBOARD WITH A PASS-THROUGH IS SITUATED IN THE CENTER OF THE ROOM, MARKING THE DISTINCTION IN TONE BETWEEN THE TWO EATING AREAS. HOWEVER, THE OPENNESS OF THE UNIT ALLOWS THE ROOM TO REMAIN UNIFIED. **Above:** BOASTING PLENTY OF SEATING, DINING SPOTS, AND WORK SURFACES, THIS LIVE-IN KITCHEN AIMS TO PLEASE. A STREAMLINED HOME-OFFICE SETUP FLOWS INTO THE KITCHEN COUNTER AND TAKES ADVANTAGE OF THE NATURAL LIGHT AFFORDED BY A LARGE WINDOW. SHELVING BEARING THE SAME VENEER AS THE DESK SURFACE ALLOWS BOOKS, DECORATIVE OBJECTS, AND A TELEVISION TO INTERMINGLE, INDICATING THAT WORK AND PLAY ARE GIVEN EQUAL FOOTING IN THIS ROOM.

Above: COLOR CAN HAVE A STRONG IMPACT IN A LIVE-IN KITCHEN. HERE, DARK GREEN CABINETRY IS JOINED BY AN ISLAND AND A TABLE THAT SPORT THE SAME PAINTED FINISH FOR A COORDINATED LOOK. BY HAVING THE TABLE ABUT THE ISLAND, THE OWNER ACHIEVES A SENSE OF INTIMACY IN THE LARGE SPACE. INTRICATELY DETAILED CHAIRS SPORTING REFRESHING BITS OF COLOR ADD A DASH OF WHIMSY, GIVING THE ROOM A LIGHTHEARTED TONE. **Opposite:** AN OPEN-LIVING FLOOR PLAN IN THIS CONTEMPORARY BEACH HOUSE PLACES THE KITCHEN FRONT AND CENTER WITH A FABULOUS VIEW. LIGHT WOOD CABINETRY AND SLEEK BLACK COUNTERS BLEND EFFORTLESSLY WITH THE LIVING AREA'S FURNISHINGS AND DECORATIVE ACCENTS.

Above: A BREAKFAST BAR JOINED BY CUSHIONED CHAIRS PROVIDES A HANDY
PLACE FOR SNACKS, QUICK MEALS, OR HOMEWORK IN THIS LIGHT-FILLED LIVE-IN
KITCHEN. WHILE THE COLOR SCHEME AND WOOD FLOORING MAKE THIS OPEN
SPACE A DECORATIVE WHOLE, THE DIFFERENT AREAS ARE SUBTLY DENOTED BY STAIRS
AND THE ARCHITECTURAL DEFINITION AT THE CEILING.

Right: THIS BEAUTIFUL INTERPRETATION OF THE GREAT ROOM FEATURES A
BRICK WALL WITH A CAPTIVATING ROUNDED WINDOW. SINCE THE KITCHEN IS
LITERALLY ON DISPLAY, HANDSOME WOODEN CABINETRY WITH A TRADITIONAL AIR
HAS BEEN CHOSEN TO GIVE THE SPACE A FORMAL FEELING, IN KEEPING WITH THE
DECOR OF THE SITTING AREA.

Above: Soothing neutrals set a peaceful tone in this live-in kitchen, where a French settee outfitted with plump cushions promises respite. Rush-seat stools at the small but serviceable island can easily be turned toward the counter or the sitting area, depending upon where the center of activity is. While easy-to-clean terra-cotta tiles grace the floor of the cooking and eating area, a sisal rug adds texture where spills are less likely.

Above: THIS LIVE-IN KITCHEN IS ACTUALLY A GREAT ROOM THAT COMBINES A FULL LIVING ROOM AND A KITCHEN IN A SINGLE SPACE. A STONE COUNTER—COMPLETE WITH SEATING—MARKS THE SEPARATION BETWEEN THE COOKING AND LIVING AREAS AND PROVIDES A PLACE FOR RELAXED MEALS. THE RUGGED STONE HEARTH AND WOOD-BEAMED CEILING CREATE A TIMELESS FEELING IN THIS FAMILY-ORIENTED ROOM.

OUTFITTING A MULTIFUNCTIONAL SPACE

Designing a live-in kitchen means more than just thinking out a good floor plan. Any kitchen can be arranged conveniently, but will it have longevity, convey a sense of style, and be easy to maintain? Furnishings and equipment make all the difference in a kitchen that is truly a live-in space.

Cabinetry is by far the predominant feature in any kitchen, but it can also be the most costly. Home-building centers and showrooms offer stock cabinets in a surprising range of styles and finishes. Many such outlets also provide professional planning and installation services. Custom-crafted cabinetry is a more expensive but often worthwhile option. Since a live-in kitchen can generally be seen from other areas of the home, its style is important to the overall decor. Custom-made cabinets can be designed with a formal appearance or strong architectural features, or even as freestanding units that look more like furniture than utilitarian cupboards.

Take a long, hard look at your existing cabinetry. Is it possible that a fresh coat of paint and different pulls or knobs could breathe new life into your kitchen? What about changing the doors? These are all cost-effective alternatives to starting from scratch, and the results can be powerful. A refreshing change of color or the relatively simple replacement of door fronts can alter the entire appearance of the kitchen.

Countertops are another important element. There are so many types of materials to choose from that cost is a primary factor. The most common countertop materials include high-tech laminates, ceramic tile, granite, wood, marble, and stainless steel. Laminates are among the less expensive alternatives, and since they come in a broad range of colors, they can suit any decorating scheme. The one drawback is that laminates do not withstand heat, so if you routinely set pots on the counter, stone or steel is a better choice.

Opposite: CHERRY CABINETRY TAKES CENTER STAGE IN THIS KITCHEN, WHICH ACHIEVES A PERFECT MARRIAGE OF FORM AND FUNCTION. THE UNUSUAL ISLAND IS THE HEIGHT OF EFFICIENCY, OFFERING STORAGE AREAS BOTH ABOVE AND BELOW ITS COUNTER. MEETING A MULTITUDE OF NEEDS, THE UNIT INCLUDES A BUILT-IN WINE RACK, CUPBOARD SPACE WITH GLASS-FRONT DOORS THAT ALLOW DISHWARE TO BE LOCATED EASILY, AND AN EXTRA SURFACE FOR SMALL APPLIANCES. THE TABLE, WHICH FITS SNUGLY INTO THE ISLAND, MAXIMIZES SPACE.

Ceramic tile is available in myriad sizes, shapes, colors, and decorative designs. Hand-painted tiles are a lovely kitchen addition when used as a backsplash. Tile is a practical countertop material because it's sturdy and heat-resistant, but dishes will shatter if dropped on it. Granite and marble countertops both exude an elegance that works in traditional and contemporary kitchens. These types of stone are highly durable, quite expensive, and prone to staining, so they should be sealed. Marble is a favorite among bakers, since it keeps pastry dough properly chilled.

Wooden countertops are seen less frequently, but they do add distinct beauty to a live-in kitchen, especially one with country styling. Generally made of hardwoods, such as maple, wooden countertops show burns and knife marks, but they are otherwise quite strong. Stainless steel, often the choice of serious chefs, is well suited to the modern or professional-style kitchen. While it can be scratched, it's easy to maintain and stain- and heat-resistant.

Kitchen flooring is also available in a wide array of materials, including vinyl, wood, tile, and stone. Vinyl flooring is an excellent selection for great rooms, thanks to its decorative versatility, affordability, durability, and low-maintenance properties. Available in both sheets and tiles, vinyl flooring comes in hundreds of different colors and patterns, including faux wood, marble, and ceramic tile.

Wood flooring can be a stunning addition to the kitchen if properly coated with a penetrating sealer and wax or a polyurethane finish. Both treatments will need to be repeated periodically to keep a wood floor water-resistant and looking its best. Oak hardwood flooring, pine planks, and parquet squares are popular choices, but an old wood floor can also be given a face-lift with a color wash or stenciled design.

Tile flooring is easy to care for, and the decorative possibilities are limitless. Unglazed tiles are preferable because their subtle texture makes the floor less likely to become slippery when wet. Borders or complementary designs can tie the spaces of a live-in kitchen together and yet give each a distinctive mark. Tile can be a sizable investment (especially to have installed), but it's well worth the cost to those who want a floor to last a lifetime. Granite, slate, and marble are very expensive, but again, the cost can be justified when you consider that the floor will endure for many years to come. Any of these three will give a live-in kitchen a classic look. Stone selected for flooring should have a somewhat textured surface and should be sealed to avoid stains.

Opposite: New isn't necessarily always best, as avid cooks who swear by their vintage stoves will relate. Here, a modern kitchen with a dining area comes to life via sunny yellow paint and an old-fashioned stove that adds a certain retro charm. The dining area, reminiscent of a sunroom, affords a refreshing view during family meals.

Outfitting a multifunctional kitchen space also means paying attention to appliances and lighting fixtures. Both should be energy-efficient, convenient to operate, and attractive. Appliances can be found with beautiful and colorful enameled finishes, such as those on the British Aga cooker; with the stainless steel finish featured on professional-quality ranges and refrigerators; and with customized finishes, such as those that echo the style of the cabinetry.

It is important that all work areas be adequately illuminated. This includes not only the surfaces where meals are prepared, but also desks and tables where paperwork or family projects are done. Options include track and recessed lighting, as well as fixtures mounted under cabinets. Hanging fixtures provide general lighting and create ambience for islands and dining areas. The lighting should reflect your decorative style, so visit several showrooms to appreciate the full scope of choices.

Left: THIS WELCOMING KITCHEN FEATURES RESILIENT FLOORING WITH A BLUE AND OCHER DIAMOND PATTERN THAT COMPLEMENTS THE GRAY-BLUE CABINETRY. A LARGE ENGLISH "DRESSER," OR HUTCH, HOLDS AN ASSORTMENT OF COLLECTIBLE DISHES AND POTTERY BOWLS. A ONE-OF-A-KIND PINE WORKTABLE HAS BEEN TRANSFORMED INTO A CONVENIENT ISLAND, COMPLETE WITH A SECOND SINK. **Above:** AN ELEGANT ISLAND BECOMES A VERY EFFICIENT WORK ZONE WHEN OUTFITTED WITH A DURABLE STONE COUNTER AND A SHINY BLACK COOKTOP. MARBLE AND GRANITE HAVE LONG BEEN APPRECIATED IN THE KITCHEN FOR THEIR INHERENT BEAUTY, EASY-CARE PROPERTIES, AND HEAT RESISTANCE.

Above: THE AMERICAN SOUTHWEST COMES TO LIFE IN THIS HIGH-SPIRITED LIVE-IN KITCHEN. A RUGGED, TIMBERED CEILING HAS SKYLIGHTS FOR NATURAL LIGHTING IN THE WORK ZONE, WHILE A WOOD-BURNING OVEN NOT ONLY GIVES FOOD A SPECIAL FLAVOR, BUT ACTS AS AN ENTICING HEARTH AS WELL. CABINETS FEATURING GLASS DOORS DISPLAY DISHWARE THAT IS IN KEEPING WITH THE HOME'S DECOR. NOTE, TOO, THE COORDINATING TILE USED FOR THE BACKSPLASHES AND THE FLOOR, WHICH CONTINUES INTO OTHER AREAS. **Opposite:** A LOG HOME IS CUSTOM-FITTED WITH AN ANGLED REFRIGERATOR AND RANGE TO ALLOW FOR AN EYE-CATCHING BANK OF WINDOWS THAT CAN BE ENJOYED FROM BOTH THE COOKING AND EATING AREAS. TO MAINTAIN THE NATURAL LOOK OF THE OPEN SPACE, AN ISLAND COMPOSED OF A RIVER ROCK BASE AND A SMOOTH, EASY-TO-CLEAN GRANITE TOP HAS BEEN INCORPORATED AS AN INTIMATE DINING AREA THAT PROVIDES EXTRA COUNTER SPACE WHEN NECESSARY. SIMILARLY STYLED CHAIRS OFFER THEIR SERVICE AT THE ISLAND AND THE MORE TRADITIONAL DINING TABLE, THEREBY UNIFYING THE LARGE ROOM.

Above: RECESSED LIGHTING AND BUILT-IN APPLIANCES MAKE THE MOST OF LIMITED KITCHEN SPACE. THIS KITCHEN/DINING AREA, DIVIDED BY A COUNTER THAT CAN BE USED FOR SNACKS AND NO-FUSS MEALS, BOASTS PAINTED CUSTOM-CRAFTED CABINETS THAT MAKE WAY FOR THE MICROWAVE AND TWIN OVENS. HERE'S PROOF POSITIVE THAT THE LIVE-IN KITCHEN CAN BE FUNCTIONAL AS WELL AS BEAUTIFUL.

Below: SETTING UP A SMALL HOME OFFICE IN A KITCHEN DOES NOT HAVE TO BE A MAJOR UNDERTAKING. HERE, A BOTTOM CUPBOARD DRAWER ACTS AS A FILE CABINET, WHILE AN ANGLED EXTENSION OF THE COUNTERTOP PROVIDES DESK SPACE. A BULLETIN BOARD AND BLACKBOARD OFFER PLENTY OF ROOM FOR MEMOS, GROCERY LISTS, AND REMINDERS OF THINGS TO DO.

Above: FORSAKING TRADITIONAL CABINETRY, THIS LIVE-IN KITCHEN HAS BEEN DESIGNED WITH A WALL OF SHELVING THAT KEEPS SPICES, ASSORTED FOODSTUFFS, AND KITCHEN EQUIPMENT WITHIN REACH. A SALVAGED TABLETOP HAS BEEN PUT TO NEW USE AS THE SURFACE FOR A SPACIOUS CENTER ISLAND.

Above: COMBINING STATE-OF-THE-ART SLEEKNESS WITH HOMEY TOUCHES, THIS LIVE-IN KITCHEN CATERS TO COOKS AND COMPANY ALIKE. A LARGE, ANGULAR, MOVABLE ISLAND OFFERS BOTH A GENEROUS WORK SPACE AND A COMFORTABLE PLACE TO EAT. CHAIRS OUTFITTED WITH PLUSH CUSHIONS FURTHER ENCOURAGE CASUAL DINING OR SIMPLY QUIET CONVERSATION WITH THE CHEF. THE COMMERCIAL PROPERTIES OF THE LARGE STAINLESS STEEL SINK UNIT AND THE PROFESSIONAL RANGE ARE TEMPERED BY WARM WOOD FLOORING AND A SOOTHING PALETTE.

Above: STATE-OF-THE-ART APPOINTMENTS CAN BE UTILIZED WITHOUT SACRIFICING THE COMFORTS OF HOME. THIS KITCHEN INCLUDES A PROFESSIONAL RANGE AND RECESSED LIGHTING FOR EFFICIENCY, TILE FLOORING AND BACKSPLASHES FOR LONGEVITY AND EASY CARE, AND HANDSOME WOOD CABINETRY FOR WARMTH. A BUILT-IN DESK FASHIONED OUT OF THE SAME MATERIALS AS THE KITCHEN CABINETS BLENDS IN SEAMLESSLY WITH THE SURROUNDINGS. WHEN DESIRED, MUSIC FILLS THE ROOM, THANKS TO SPEAKERS PERCHED INCONSPICUOUSLY ATOP THE CABINETS.

Above: WITH THE ADDITION OF A LARGE ISLAND BOASTING DUAL SINKS, A BOOKCASE TO HOUSE FAVORITE NOVELS AND COOKBOOKS, AND DECORATIVE LIGHT FIXTURES DIRECTLY ABOVE THE WORK SPACE, THIS KITCHEN BECAME A SMASHING SUCCESS. A VAST WINDOW IN THE EATING AREA TAKES ADVANTAGE OF A SPECTACULAR VIEW, MAKING THIS SPACE NOT ONLY AN APPEALING DINING AREA, BUT AN ENTICING GATHERING SPOT IN GENERAL.

Above: THIS SIZABLE LIVE-IN KITCHEN HAS A TASTEFUL, CLEAN LOOK THANKS TO ITS SIMPLE WHITE CABINETRY, WHICH BLENDS IN WITH THE BUILT-IN SOFA. A TWO-TONED TABLE TAKES THE PLACE OF AN ISLAND, PERFORMING DOUBLE DUTY AS AN EATING SPACE AND A WORKSTATION. RECESSED SPACES HAVE BEEN CLEVERLY INCORPORATED INTO THE ROOM'S DESIGN TO SHOWCASE SELECT POTTERY PIECES BEARING HUES SIMILAR TO THOSE OF THE TOSS PILLOWS ON THE SOFA AND THE AREA RUG BENEATH THE TABLE. THE OVERALL EFFECT IS ONE OF SOPHISTICATED HARMONY.

Above: A COMFORTABLE BANQUETTE TAKES ADVANTAGE OF THE VIEW FROM THIS LIVE-IN KITCHEN. THANKS TO IMMENSE WINDOWS AND A DOOR FITTED WITH GLASS PANES, THE OUTDOOR SETTING BECOMES PART OF THE DECOR. **Opposite:** TRADITIONAL STYLE GETS A FRESH TREATMENT IN THIS OPEN KITCHEN WITH ITS BLUE AND WHITE STRIPED WALLPAPER, WHITE GLASS-FRONT CABINETRY, AND DECORATIVE BACKSPLASH TILES. OPENING ONTO A DECK, THE DINING AREA FEATURES HARDWOOD FLOORING AND A HANDSOME WOODEN TABLE WITH WICKER CHAIRS THAT ENHANCE THE ROOM'S BREEZY FEELING.

Left: A BEIGE LAMINATE COUNTERTOP IS USED ON AN ISLAND THAT ALSO DOUBLES AS A BREAKFAST BAR. SPECIAL TOUCHES, SUCH AS CORNER SHELVES AND A TAMBOUR SLIDING DOOR THAT HIDES SMALL APPLIANCES, HELP TO INCREASE THE AMOUNT OF STORAGE SPACE AND ACHIEVE AN UNCLUTTERED LOOK. MATCHING LIGHTING FIXTURES TURN A NECESSITY INTO A DECORATIVE STATEMENT.

Opposite: A LIBERAL USE OF COLOR CREATES A FESTIVE ATMOSPHERE IN THIS SPIRITED KITCHEN. VIBRANT HUES AND LOW-MAINTENANCE SURFACES, SUCH AS TILE FLOORING, A MOSAIC BACKSPLASH, AND LAMINATE COUNTERS, MAKE THIS SPACE EASY TO KEEP CLEAN AND PLEASURABLE TO WORK IN. ON THE ISLAND, TROMPE L'OEIL CUPBOARDS DISPLAYING A COLLECTION OF BRIGHT DISHES ADD A PLAYFUL NOTE.

DECORATIVE STYLES

Today's kitchen is every bit as stylish and alluring as any other room in the home. The live-in kitchen, in fact, may be the best place to salute a particular decorative style, given the myriad colors, materials, and textures available to help you create the subtle essence, or bolder stance, of an interior design scheme.

What's your personal decorating style? Take a close look at the other rooms in your home, and consider the way you live. Perhaps you've surrounded yourself with natural textures and country checks, or maybe you prefer a more sleek and streamlined look. The colors you love, the furnishings you cherish, and the fabrics you find appealing all help determine direction when it comes to interior design. The most popular decorative styles for the live-in kitchen include traditional, country, Victorian Revival, European, and contemporary.

Traditional style calls upon time-honored classics to fashion a look with long-lasting appeal. A wide range of colors can be called into use, from basic whites and neutrals to pastels and darker hues. Such elegant materials as tile, granite, marble, and slate help impart the spirit of the style. Attention to architectural details, such as crown moldings on cabinetry and ceilings, will add a bit of formal flair. Striped fabrics, large florals, and pictorials such as toiles de Jouy are ideal for upholstery and window treatments. For the dining area, consider Queen Anne, Chippendale, neoclassical, Shaker, or Arts and Crafts furniture designs. Gilt-framed artwork, fresh flowers, and porcelain jars make perfect decorative accents.

Country style, which can be interpreted in many different ways, has become a favorite for creating interiors that offer comfort, simplified living, and relaxed good looks. Country can be rustic, with wood-beamed ceilings, walls of unhewn logs, and painted cabinetry, or even a tad elegant, with warm wooden furnishings and white cabinets. The live-in kitchen with a country decorating theme can showcase natural or painted wooden cabinetry with brass, porcelain, or wooden pulls. White walls allow furnishings and decorative elements to stand out (for a more modern country look), or a vibrant, old-fashioned

Opposite: THIS UPDATED VERSION OF A EUROPEAN LIVE-IN KITCHEN MAKES GOOD USE OF PINE CABINETRY AND FRENCH-INSPIRED FURNISHINGS TO CREATE OLD-WORLD APPEAL. LOVELY PROVENÇAL RUSH-SEAT CHAIRS PULL UP TO A ROUND TABLE BEDECKED WITH A FLORAL TABLECLOTH AND MINIATURE BOUQUETS OF FRESH FLOWERS.

hue can be selected to create a traditional country mood. Wallpapers with mini prints, stripes, or checks are also strong contenders in a country setting. Flooring can be pine planks, hardwood, tile, or vinyl with an old-time look. For dining, a rectangular pine table, a round oak table, or a drop-leaf table can be surrounded by a variety of seating options. Sturdy benches, Windsor chairs, and slat-back chairs with rush seats are all good choices. Add a wrought-iron chandelier with graceful arms, and let the natural light in. Windows with a view can be left bare or dressed with simple shades, tab curtains, or decorative valances for added country charm.

Victorian Revival style is especially beautiful in a live-in kitchen, where white or dark wooden cabinetry with glass-front doors is reminiscent of the nineteenth-century butler's pantry. A backdrop of soft, muted hues, beadboard wainscoting, and floral wallpaper creates the essence of the style. Hardwood and parquet flooring, as well as tile or a resilient flooring with a period theme, are suitable options underfoot. Handsome furnishings made of cherry, mahogany, or walnut are perfect for dining, while a sitting area can be outfitted with chintz-covered easy chairs, a lovely wood-trimmed sofa, and tasseled throw pillows. Use delicate and airy lace panels at the windows, and add a bright note with lamps sporting frosted, etched, or art glass shades.

The vibrant colors of the French countryside are often the inspiration for a live-in kitchen with a European demeanor. Walls washed or painted in such colors as sunflower yellow, ocher, terra-cotta, lavender, olive, russet, or French blue can be accompanied by freestanding cupboards and baker's racks for an "unfitted" look recalling a peaceful, rural lifestyle. If built-in cabinetry is preferred, honey pine cupboards will do quite nicely, and a striking armoire can be added for additional storage and a strong sense of style. Floors can be set with terra-cotta or colorful ceramic tiles to add rustic texture, and counters can be fitted with tiles or wood. Introduce French country furnishings, such as ladder-back chairs with rush seats and a rectangular pine table. For smaller dining spaces, a metal bistro table with matching chairs will go a long way in achieving the desired tone. Add cushions and curtains made with a Provençal print or a toile de Jouy pattern to complete the look.

The contemporary or modern live-in kitchen can be geared toward a minimalist, professional look, or it can have a sophisticated air. A neutral palette allows blond wooden cabinetry to set the tone. A generous addition of stainless steel counters and appliances, granite or marble counters, glass blocks used as half-walls or shelves, or black appliances and laminate counters will contribute modern appeal. The entire look is sleek, crisp, and clean; clutter does not exist in a contemporary kitchen, as small appliances and other necessities are kept out of sight, hidden behind cupboard doors. Recessed and track lighting are favored over obvious fixtures. Furnishings in a dining or sitting area should have a cutting-edge look but offer solid comfort.

Right: THIS THOROUGHLY MOD-
ERN LIVE-IN KITCHEN COMBINES
ARCHITECTURAL FLAIR WITH STAINLESS
STEEL COUNTERS AND WOOD CABI-
NETRY. THE USE OF SHELVING RATHER
THAN WALL-HUNG CUPBOARDS REIN-
FORCES THE AIRY FEELING OF THE
SPACE. THIS SENSATION IS FURTHER
ENHANCED BY THE WHITE AND
BLOND COLOR SCHEME, WHICH
EXTENDS TO THE COUCH.
SYMMETRICALLY ARRANGED UNITS AT
EITHER END OF THE KITCHEN HOUSE
THE REFRIGERATOR, MICROWAVE,
AND OVEN, CREATING A REASSUR-
ING SENSE OF BALANCE.

Above: IN THIS LIVE-IN KITCHEN, SIMPLE WHITE CABINETRY IS MADE MORE ELEGANT BY ADDING A NOTABLE CROWN MOLDING. A CENTER ISLAND WITH A RICH GRANITE COUNTERTOP IS ACCESSORIZED WITH SHAKER-STYLE CHAIRS FOR CASUAL MEALS. **Opposite:** AT THE OTHER END OF THE SAME ROOM, A MORE FORMAL DINING AREA FURTHER DISPLAYS THE BEAUTY AND SIMPLICITY OF SHAKER DESIGN. A LONG DINING TABLE IS JOINED BY A SHAKER-STYLE BENCH AND RED AND WHITE TAPE CHAIRS THAT ARE SIMILAR TO THE ONES AT THE ISLAND. THE UNDERSTATED HEARTH PROVIDES A GLORIOUS FOCAL POINT, WHILE SELECT ACCESSORIES—THE RED RUG, WROUGHT-IRON CHANDELIER, AND BASKETS—REINFORCE THE DECORATIVE THEME.

Left: WHITE CABINETRY, TERRA-COTTA FLOORING, AND A COLORFUL TILE BACKSPLASH PROVIDE THE PERFECT BACKDROP FOR A RUSTIC WOODEN TABLE AND RUSH-SEAT CHAIRS IN THIS MODERN INTERPRETATION OF A COUNTRY KITCHEN. SUCH COLORFUL ACCENTS AS THE AREA RUG, THE TABLE RUNNER, AND THE RED ENAMELED POT ON THE STOVE CONTRIBUTE COUNTRY CHARM. THE PERFECT FINISHING TOUCH IS THE PITCHER FILLED WITH FLOWERS THAT ACTS AS A CENTERPIECE. **Opposite:** PAYING TRIBUTE TO THE COLONIAL PAST, THIS HIGH-STYLE COUNTRY KITCHEN COMBINES REFINED, DEEP BLUE-GREEN CABINETRY WITH WARM WOOD FLOORING AND BUTCHER-BLOCK COUNTERTOPS. A WOODEN TABLE IS JOINED BY WINDSOR CHAIRS, WHILE A PERIOD-PERFECT CHANDELIER PRESIDES OVERHEAD.

Opposite: OLD-WORLD CHARM HAS BEEN CALLED UPON TO FASHION A LOVELY "UNFITTED" KITCHEN. A LARGE, FREESTANDING HUTCH WITH CREAM-COLORED PAINT IS JOINED BY A DESK THAT HAS PLENTY OF SPACE FOR STORING COOKBOOKS AND PERFORMING PAPERWORK. IN ADDITION, A EUROPEAN STYLE SINK HAS BEEN SET INTO A HANDSOME UNIT WITH A STONE COUNTERTOP. BY INCORPORATING SEVERAL FURNITURE PIECES AS STORAGE FOR NECESSARY ITEMS, THE KITCHEN EMBRACES THE IDEA THAT IT IS MUCH MORE THAN JUST A COOKING FACILITY. **Above:** IN THIS MULTIPURPOSE SPACE, TRADITIONAL TOUCHES ARE JUXTAPOSED WITH MODERN COMPONENTS. HARDWOOD FLOORING, STRIPED VALANCES, AND CANDLESTICK WALL SCONCES PAIRED WITH A MATCHING CHANDELIER CARRY THE TRADITIONAL TONE OF THE CABINETRY INTO THE DINING AREA, WHILE A METAL CHAIR FROM THE DINING SET FINDS A NEW HOME AT THE KITCHEN ISLAND.

Above: DECORATIVE DETAILS CAN TRANSFORM AN ISLAND INTO THE STAR ATTRACTION OF A LIVE-IN KITCHEN. HERE, A PERIOD CABINET WITH LOVELY CARVINGS BECOMES AN EYE-CATCHING ISLAND EQUIPPED WITH A SECOND SINK. AN IRON CHANDELIER WITH MINIATURE CANDLESTICK LAMPS AND A RED AND WHITE BALLOON SHADE AT THE WINDOW ENHANCE THE TRADITIONAL TONE OF THE SURROUNDINGS.

Left: CHEERFUL AND HEART-WARMING, THIS UPDATED VERSION OF A COUNTRY KITCHEN BOASTS WOOD FLOORING, A BAMBOO WINDOW SHADE, AND RUSTIC STOOLS, ALL OF WHICH HELP ESTABLISH THE PROVINCIAL TONE. WHITE GLASS-FRONT CABINETS AND AN ISLAND BEARING BEADBOARD PANELS ARE IN KEEPING WITH THE STYLE, OFFERING A CASUAL ELEGANCE THAT IS REFLECTED IN THE OVERSTUFFED COUCH. **Opposite:** LESS IS DEFINITELY MORE IN THIS COUNTRY KITCHEN, WHERE JUST A FEW WELL-CHOSEN ELEMENTS EFFECTIVELY CONVEY THE SPIRIT OF THE STYLE. SUNNY YELLOW PAINT AND WHITE BEADBOARD PANELING PROVIDE AN UPLIFTING BACKDROP, WHILE A HARVEST TABLE AND AN ASSORTMENT OF WINDSOR CHAIRS GIVE THE ROOM A RELAXED TONE. A CURVED-ARM CHANDELIER, A CASUAL AREA RUG, AND AN ARRAY OF PASTEL DISHWARE SUBTLY CONTRIBUTE TO THE HOMEY FEELING OF THE SPACE.

Above: SLEEK, LIGHT WOODEN CABINETRY, A BLACK RANGE, AND A STAINLESS STEEL REFRIGERATOR HAVE BEEN SELECTED TO OUTFIT THIS CONTEMPORARY KITCHEN. GLASS-FRONT CUPBOARD DOORS THAT SHOW OFF STEMWARE AND DISHES, A DECORATIVE LIGHTING FIXTURE, AND A METAL TABLE WITH STOOLS MAKE THIS SPACE MORE INVITING. COLORFUL LINENS AND AN ATTRACTIVE POTTERY BOWL DESIGNATED FOR FRUIT ADD A PERSONAL NOTE.

Above: A CONTEMPORARY ARCHITECTURAL DESIGN AND CUSTOM-CRAFTED CABINETRY TAKE CENTER STAGE IN THIS SPACIOUS LIVE-IN KITCHEN. WOOD FLOORING, A PANORAMIC VIEW, AND A STATE-OF-THE-ART WORK AREA WHERE APPLIANCES ARE FLUSH WITH THE CABINETS CREATE A DECORATIVE AND HIGHLY FUNCTIONAL FAMILY-BASED ROOM.

Left: This contemporary kitchen achieves decorative flair by incorporating open metal-and-wood shelves to display a collection of ceramic pieces and colored glassware. The curves of the island, stools, and footed armchair wittily echo the shapely pottery. A television that provides entertainment for the cook is camouflaged by a wooden case. **Above:** A stainless steel island with a butcher-block top makes a striking addition to this contemporary kitchen. In keeping with the spirit of the style, clutter is nonexistent, but select accessories—a bouquet of fragrant lilies and a bowl of fruit—are added to give the room warmth.

Adding That Personal Touch

A great deal of thought, planning, and sometimes expense goes into designing a live-in kitchen to suit your needs and make your home a true haven. After the building, remodeling, or sprucing up has been done and you've decorated and furnished the space, you'll want it to reflect your personality. The most beautiful and well-appointed kitchen will still come up short if it doesn't have that personal touch. To make any kitchen warm and hospitable so that family and friends will want to linger, turn your attention to the little details.

Obviously the kitchen needs to be equipped with cookware, dishes, linens, and so on, but how such items are stored—or displayed—can make a decorative difference. For example, heirloom china, flea market finds, or everyday dishes can be displayed in a vintage cupboard, or a plate rail can be used to showcase favorite pieces. Plates also make attractive wall art—metal hangers can be used to arrange a selection of chintz china, blue and white Staffordshire, or white ironstone on a wall. Wall-hung plate racks, long a staple in the European kitchen, can be used instead of cabinets to show off dishes, or cupboards without doors may be preferred for a more rustic look. For any avid collector, the problem is often using restraint rather than suffering from a lack of items to display. Those with an abundance of kitchen tools, china, and pottery can store some items and change displays occasionally rather than overflowing the kitchen with things.

Cookware isn't just functional—it can also be surprisingly decorative. Serious cooks have long favored copper pots and pans for their ability to distribute heat evenly, and it's a shame to hide such gleaming beauty behind a cupboard door. Rather, consider suspending an iron or stainless steel rack from the ceiling above the range or

Opposite: Proving that the kitchen is the heart of the home, this great room pulls out all the stops. Dried flowers hang from ceiling beams, as well as from the mantel, reflecting a passion for gardening. Continuing this theme, a stenciled border on the far wall bears a floral design that picks up the hues in the tile edging of the counter. The handpainted inscription on the fireplace makes all those who enter feel special.

island to keep cookware within arm's reach and to enjoy its handsome looks.

If your kitchen has a window with a generous ledge and you happen to be cultivating a green thumb, container gardening is a wonderful way to bring freshness and beauty into the space. Window boxes and colorful ceramic or terra-cotta pots also lend a personal touch to the kitchen when filled with topiaries, flowers, or herbs that you can snip for cooking. And it needn't stop there: fill a vase, an old enamel coffeepot, or a stoneware jug with fresh flowers and use it as a centerpiece on the table or as part of a tabletop vignette in the sitting area.

While countertops in any kitchen shouldn't be filled to the point that they appear cluttered, you can still keep necessities close at hand and arrange them in artful displays. Cluster attractive bottles of oils and vinegars in a wire basket, or place frequently used utensils in a colorful piece of pottery or a decorative tin. A one-of-a-kind wooden or glass bowl can keep fruit and vegetables close by and create a lovely still life at the same time.

Look above your kitchen cabinetry. Is there space between the wall-hung cupboards and the ceiling? If so, you have just found the perfect spot for your basket collection. This is also a lovely, out-of-the-way space to showcase a collection of antique platters, ceramic pitchers, or vintage coffee tins.

Now examine your live-in kitchen as a whole. Just as you've added notable decorative details in the cooking area, you'll want to put a personal stamp on the dining or living area. Art is a highly personal matter and therefore a good way to express individuality. Adorn your walls with those select pieces that give you immense pleasure. Freestanding cupboards or built-in bookshelves in a dining or sitting area make space available for much more than just books. Add warmth to the live-in kitchen by grouping family photos on a shelf, bring together that collection of silver or brass candlesticks for eye-catching impact, or cluster small, cherished objects for decorative appeal. If you are fortunate enough to have a fireplace in the live-in kitchen, design a mantelscape with a few favorite possessions.

Add color, texture, and coziness to a live-in kitchen with area rugs. Oriental, needlepoint, and colorful textured rugs or sisal matting can define the dining space and add comfort underfoot in work zones. Rugs can also help convey style and give a contemporary setting a softer edge.

Last but far from least, keep your decorative style in mind when selecting accessories to personalize your live-in kitchen. While vintage objects can often be juxtaposed with contemporary surroundings, some items will seem hopelessly lost and out of place when added to a specific period or regional decor. Baskets, wooden bowls, and graniteware make fitting statements in a country-style kitchen, but they would seem out of character in the Victorian kitchen reminiscent of a butler's pantry.

Right: CONTEMPORARY SPACES NEEDN'T BE AUSTERE; SUBTLE INFUSIONS OF COLOR AND TEXTURE CAN HIGHLIGHT THE BEAUTY OF CLEAN LINES AND SMOOTH SURFACES WHILE ADDING WARMTH TO A ROOM. HERE, A MODERN KITCHEN AND DINING TABLE ARE JUXTAPOSED WITH RUSTIC TWIG CHAIRS THAT PROVIDE A NICE CONTRAST IN TEXTURE. TILES BEARING MUTED SPLASHES OF COLOR THAT RESEMBLE PAINTBRUSH STROKES GIVE THE ROOM AN ARTISTIC AIR.

Above: THIS KITCHEN CELEBRATES THE OWNER'S LOVE OF FOLK ART. HANDMADE DOLLS, CARVED ANIMALS, AND A BEAUTIFUL INDIAN TAPESTRY ADD WARMTH AND PERSONAL TOUCHES TO THE SPACIOUS ROOM. **Opposite:** ATTENTION TO DETAIL IS EVIDENT IN THIS INSPIRING KITCHEN. THE WALL-HUNG CUPBOARDS ARE LEFT DOORLESS TO SHOW OFF THE COPPER COOKWARE, WHILE A STEP-BACK CUPBOARD DISPLAYS A COLLECTION OF FINE CHINA. AN OLD CROCK NEAR THE STOVE KEEPS UTENSILS IN ONE PLACE, AND AN ORNATE TABLE SERVING AS AN ISLAND HOLDS FRESH PRODUCE. NOTE, TOO, THE TILED "AREA RUG" UNDER THE TABLE.

Opposite: A LIVE-IN KITCHEN IN A CITY APARTMENT BECOMES A WELCOMING SPACE, THANKS TO THE ADDITION OF BELOVED ITEMS. OPEN SHELVES SHOW OFF SKILLFULLY ARRANGED DISHWARE, WHILE WHIMSICAL PIECES OF ARTWORK PREVENT THE EXPANSE ABOVE FROM SEEMING TOO BARE AND IMPERSONAL. AN ALMOST OVERFLOWING DISPLAY CABINET IS STRATEGICALLY SITUATED SO THAT ITS CONTENTS CAN BE ENJOYED BY AUDIENCES IN BOTH THE COOKING AND EATING AREAS.

Above: THE SPACE ATOP WALL-HUNG CABINETS IS IDEAL FOR MAKING A PERSONAL STATEMENT. CERAMIC CANISTERS, POTTERY PIECES, AND EVEN A COW OR TWO HOLD PRIDE OF PLACE IN THIS HANDSOME KITCHEN. ADD AN ARRAY OF WALL-HUNG MAJOLICA PLATES AND A VINTAGE BREAD BOX, AND THE KITCHEN BECOMES A GALLERY FOR COLLECTIBLES. THIS ENTHUSIASM FOR UNUSUAL OBJECTS IS FURTHER EVIDENCED BY THE ASSORTMENT OF DECORATIVE PLATES ADORNING THE EATING SURFACE.

Below: FRENCH DOORS ARE OPENED WIDE SO THAT THE OUTSIDE GREENERY CAN BE VIEWED FROM THIS KITCHEN/DINING AREA. INSTEAD OF SURROUNDING THE TABLE WITH LIKE CHAIRS, THE OWNERS HAVE INCORPORATED A PRIZED ANTIQUE BENCH THAT WOULD LOOK EQUALLY AT HOME ON A FRONT PORCH, THEREBY TYING TOGETHER THE OUTDOORS AND THE INTERIOR. A CANDELABRA ATOP THE TABLE ADDS OLD-WORLD ELEGANCE TO THE CASUAL "ALFRESCO" SURROUNDINGS. **Opposite:** HOMEY ELEMENTS THROUGHOUT THIS QUINTESSENTIAL COUNTRY KITCHEN ADD STYLE AND CHARM. AN OVAL BRAIDED RUG, A CHECKERED TABLECLOTH, AND A MINI-CHECK, FABRIC WINDOW SHADE PROVIDE SOFTENING TOUCHES. THANKS TO A BOUQUET OF RED GERANIUMS AND A BLUE AND WHITE PITCHER FILLED WITH SPRING BLOOMS, THE KITCHEN BECOMES A PERSONAL TRIBUTE TO THE BEAUTY OF NATURE AND THE POWER OF CHERISHED ITEMS FROM THE PAST.

Above: A BOUQUET OF WHITE TULIPS AND A PAIR OF WHITE CANDLES ADD A TOUCH OF REFINEMENT TO A BOISTEROUS HAND-PAINTED KITCHEN TABLE. THE TABLE IS THE PERFECT PLACE FOR A LITTLE ONE TO DRAW OR DO HOMEWORK WHILE THE ADULTS COOK. OVERHEAD, A PAINTED GREEN RACK SHOWS OFF COPPER COOKWARE.

Above: WHEN INJECTING A LIVE-IN KITCHEN WITH PERSONALITY, ONE MUST CONSIDER HOW DECORATIVE ITEMS WILL BE DISPLAYED. HERE, SHELVES MOUNTED ABOVE A DESK SHOWCASE A COLORFUL ARRAY OF CERAMICS THAT NOT ONLY CREATES AN UPLIFTING WORK ENVIRONMENT, BUT BRIGHTENS UP THE ROOM IN GENERAL. HIGHLY PRACTICAL, THESE SAME SHELVES PLACE BOOKS WITHIN EASY REACH OF THE DESK AND HOUSE A SMALL TELEVISION THAT CAN BE WATCHED FROM OTHER AREAS OF THE ROOM. A LEDGE RUNNING ABOVE THE SHELVES, DOORWAY, AND CABINETRY BOASTS ADDITIONAL COLLECTIBLES, DRAWING THE EYE UPWARD. **Right:** OPEN SHELVING PROVES IDEAL FOR TAMING A COLLECTION OF FAVORITE ITEMS. HERE, AN ARTFUL ARRANGEMENT OF BOTTLES, DISHES, AND GLASSWARE CREATES A FOCAL POINT THAT GIVES THE LIVE-IN KITCHEN A SIGNATURE TOUCH.

Sources

**RETAILERS AND
MANUFACTURERS**

American Olean Tile Co.
1000 N. Cannon Avenue
Lansdale, PA 19446
(215) 855-1111
www.aotile.com

Ann Sacks Tile & Stone
P.O. Box 3859
Portland, OR 97208
(800) 278-8453
www.annsacks.com
*Call for catalog and location
of nearest retailer.*

Armstrong World Industries,
    Inc.
P.O. Box 3001
Lancaster, PA 17604
(717) 397-0611
(800) 233-3823
www.armstrongfloors.com
Flooring.

The Chuctanunda Co.
One 4th Avenue
Amsterdam, NY 12010
(518) 843-3983
*Antique European enamel-
ware for the kitchen and bath.
Call or write for brochure and
show schedule. Does a large
mail-order business.*

Contour Kitchen Design
1128 Mainland Road
Vancouver, British Columbia
V6B 5L1 Canada
(604) 682-0545
Cabinetry and appliances.

Country Floors
15 E. 16th Street
New York, NY 10003
(212) 627-8300
Ceramic tile. Call for catalog.

Country Tinware
RR 1, Box 73
Mt. Pleasant Mills, PA 17853
(800) 800-4846
*Candleholders, wall sconces,
and lanterns. Call for catalog.*

Crate & Barrel
P.O. Box 9059
Wheeling, IL 60090
(800) 451-8217
*Furnishings, modular units,
specialty items. Call for
catalog and location of
nearest store.*

Ethan Allen
P.O. Box 1966
Danbury, CT 06813-1966
(800) 228-9229
(203) 743-8000
www.ethanallen.com
*Furnishings. Call for catalog
and location of nearest store.*

Hanover Kitchens
79 Shepherd Avenue West
North York, Ontario
M2N 1M4 Canada
(416) 512-7979
Kitchen renovations.

The Kennebec Company
1 Front Street
Bath, ME 04530
(207) 443-2131
*Custom cabinetry designs for
the kitchen. Call or write
for catalog.*

The Kitchen Emporium
54 Kent Street
Woodstock, Ontario
N4S 6Y7 Canada
(519) 537-7180
*Cabinetry, countertops,
hardware.*

The Kitchen Place
861 Simco Street South
Oshawa, Ontario L1H 4K8
Canada
(905) 579-2417
*Cabinetry, countertops, sinks,
faucets.*

Mannington Floors
P.O. Box 30
Salem, NJ 08079
(800) 356-6787
*Vinyl and laminate flooring.
Call for product brochure and
location of nearest retailer.*

Northern Refrigerator
    Company
21149 Northland Drive
P.O. Box 204
Paris, MI 49307
*Specializes in reproduction
icebox style refrigerators for
an authentic look in the
Victorian kitchen. Write
for information regarding
product.*

Plain & Fancy Custom
   Cabinetry
P.O. Box 519
Schaefferstown, PA 17088
(717) 949-6571
Call for catalog.

Rutt Custom Cabinetry
1564 Main Street
P.O. Box 129
Goodville, PA 17528
(800) 706-7888
www.rutt1.com

Thomasville Furniture
P.O. Box 339
Thomasville, NC 27361
(800) 225-0265
*Call for brochure and location
of nearest store.*

Town & Country Kitchens
17212 107th Avenue
Edmonton, Alberta T5S 1E9
Canada
(780) 489-3331
Cabinetry.

PHOTOGRAPHY CREDITS

©Steven Brooke: 68 left

©Grey Crawford: 19, 65

©Carlos Domenech: 8 (designer: Jennifer
Garrigues); 14, 39 (architect: Taylor &
Taylor); 54 (designer: Marco Guinaldo);
55 (architect: Robert Florez)

©Michael Garland: 13 (architect:
Marshall Lewis Architecture); 28–29
(designer: Joe Ruggiero Designs)

©Steve Gross & Susan Daley: 6, 24, 53,
64, 66 right

©Nancy Hill: 10, 16 (designer: Scott
Grandis of Living Spaces, Inc.); 15
(designer: Karyne Johnson of Panache
Interiors); 32 (designer: Deborah T.
Lipner); 36, 50, 51 left (designer: Kitchens
by Deane); 37 (architect: Robert Nevins,
AIA)

Inside: ©J. Caillaut: 33 left

©Michael Jensen: 38 (architect: Prentiss
Architects)

©David Livingston: 9, 20 left, 20–21, 22,
29 right, 35, 48, 49, 62, 63, 66 left; 2,
18, 23 (designer: Stone Wood); 12
(designer: Robert Nebolon); 33 right, 57
right (designer: Eugene Nahemow); 40
(designer: Kitchens & More); 51 right
(designer: Alice Wiley); 61 (designer:
De Sousa Hughes)

©Deborah Mazzoleni: 42, 46, 47; 41
(designer: Nancy Poole)

©Brad Simmons: 31 (architect: Don
Briemhurst of Home Field Advantage);
58 (builder: Ralph Williamson); 67
(designer: Leigh Waller)

©William Stites: 68–69

©Dominique Vorillon: 30; 17 (architect:
Kajer); 27 (architect: Fung & Blatt);
34 (designer: Tom Douglas); 45 (architect:
Biben/Bosley); 52 (designer: Kimberly
Latham Design); 56–57 (designer: Sallie
Trout)

INDEX